The Legacy of Geneva

The Gift of a Mother's Wisdom

Kolean W. Sanders

ACKNOWLEDGMENTS

Thank you to all the angels God has
put in my path over the years to help me in
my quest for life and survival.
I am most grateful for your words
of encouragement, vision for the future,
wisdom in the midst of my quandaries,
or just your listening ear.
You have no idea how much I have
gained from you nor how much
I appreciate you.

Thank you Mom for being able to see and
understand me better than I could for myself,
and for preparing me for some
of life's most difficult courses.

Thank you to all who contributed to this volume,
By scribing, illustrating, and proofreading.

You are very much
a part of my journey.

Copyright © 2017 Kolean W. Sanders
All rights reserved.
ISBN: 1974559653
ISBN-13: 978-1974559657

If ye shall ask anything

IN MY NAME,

I WILL DO IT

--John 14:14

KOLEAN W SANDERS

DEDICATION

To Linda, Cedric, Kolleana and Harmonee.

May the legacy continue.

KOLEAN W SANDERS

TABLE OF CONTENTS

Introduction

1 “Planting seeds today for a better tomorrow.”

2 “If there are ten women in the room, always be the lady.”

3 “Always be your very best; that will be good enough.”

4 “Stay on the road less traveled by; not many are on that road.”

5 “All ladies that have a husband are your sisters; they should have the same respect”

6 “Always know that where there is darkness, I will make sure you have light.”

TABLE OF CONTENTS

7   "You will give away money, houses, jewelry, and clothes. Your cup will run over."

8   "Walk for your brothers and sisters until they can walk for themselves."

9   "Be careful of your tongue; it cuts like a knife. Once you cut someone, the healing will take time, or the wound may be too deep to heal."

10   "Listen to God when He speaks to you. Do what He says and don't be afraid."

11   "You will meet people many, many years later who will remind you of these conversations, in words, or a smile. They will look into your eyes and say 'wow!', and you will feel my presence."

12   Conclusion

INTRODUCTION

With gratitude I have benefitted from the wisdom of my mother. As I look into the rear-view mirror at the journey of my life and reflect on, the good, the bad, the sweet and the bitter, I should be a very bad person. In fact, I know that I am not supposed to even be here. I would not but for the grace and mercy of God and the patient, loving care of my dear mother.

At times, I stand overwhelmed and amazed at the foresight of this woman. Thanks to my mother and the legacy of wisdom she poured into me, I was given the option to choose another path!.

I have relied on Mom's precepts throughout my life and have shared her wisdom with others countless times. It is my prayer that my own life will bring honor to God, and in some way reflect this legacy imparted to me.

In my experience, I have found that many women, like me, have lived through one or more of the nine types of violence or abuse:

- Physical violence,
- Sexual violence,
- Emotional violence,

- Psychological violence,
- Cultural violence,
- Verbal abuse,
- Neglect,
- Financial abuse,
- And even spiritual (or religious) abuse.

They all contain the same meaning: "<u>Control</u>!"

Once, I started to re-define my life, I realized that my power was the ability and the responsibility to say "NO" and to take control of my own life!!

My mother empowered me with the tools to succeed with principles like: how to plant seeds, and staying on the road less traveled by, always being a lady, and so much more.

I hope as you read this booklet, you will find comfort in knowing you are never alone. You should know that, naturally and supernaturally, the power is inside of you!

Second Corinthians 12:9 (ESV) states, But he said to me, "My grace is sufficient for you, for my power is made perfect in weakness. Therefore I will boast all the more gladly of my weaknesses, so that the power of Christ may rest upon me."

Your acknowledgement of the five basic life stages of growth and recovery will help to lead you out of the darkness into the light.

1. SHOCK: "How can this happen to me?" or "What did I do to deserve this?" Feeling inadequate, ashamed, questioning your self-worth, and maybe even feeling guilty.

2. ANGER at the people causing hurt and pain in your life, feeling angry at yourself and becoming self-critical, saying If I could have, would have, or should have, and speaking negativity into your life.

3. BARGAINING your life and wishes, and wishing that things could be different. Cheating yourself out of opportunity, self-sabotage, deliberately destroying your reputation, in case your attempts to compromise fail, giving up.

4. DEPRESSION comes by focusing on your situation. You may become frustrated, silent, withdraw, and doubt yourself. You may feel hurt and that no one cares what happened to you.

5. Once you acknowledge, accept, and take responsibility, you learn ACCEPTANCE: What happened is in the past, and it is an experience; a lesson you should learn from. It is important then to move forward.

Take time to analyze the situation. Then be the voice to help someone else through their journey. Get excited about your life and "Plant Seeds Today for A Better Tomorrow", because someone needs your experiences to move them forward and into a better life!

Remember, our lives are not about us. It's about what we do for others. My mother said you should pray for the people who hurt and disrespected you; (if only you could take your eyes off yourselves, and put them on someone else), and watch how God shows up for you!

I pray this for you as you read this booklet, and as you feel or recognize any form of abuse that you witnessed or experienced:

God teach us to "let the peace that comes from Christ rule in our hearts." (Col. 3:15) When I forgive in words, allow your Holy Spirit to fill my heart with peace. I pray this peace which only comes from Jesus will rule in my heart, keeping out doubt and questions. And above all, I am thankful, not just today, not just this week, but always. Thank you for the reminder, "Always be thankful." (Col. 3:15) With gratitude I can draw closer to You and let go of unforgiveness. With gratitude I can see the person who caused my pain as a child of the Most High God; loved and accepted. Help me find the compassion that comes with true forgiveness.

In Jesus' name, Amen.

I wish blessing to all who read this booklet.

Kolean W Sanders

1

PLANTING SEEDS TODAY
FOR A BETTER TOMORROW

> **But I say unto you which hear, Love your enemies, do good to them which hate you, bless them that curse you, and pray for them which despitefully use you. And unto him that strikes thee on the one cheek, offer also the other; and him that taketh away thy cloak forbid not to take thy coat also. Luke 6:27-29**

When I was in school growing up, I had my own bully, whose name I will withhold. But I will never forget her and how the two of us got along.

Since my hair was very long, my mother often spent a lot of

time managing it. When I went to school, my mother would have my hair braided up pretty. She would adorn me with ribbons and barrettes.

This bully would take down all my braids, confiscate my accessories, and throw my hair anyway she wanted. She would have me just looking a mess as I left school and went back to the house. The next day I would see this bully wearing my ribbons.

Upon seeing me in disarray, my mother would always ask, "What happened to you?" I would answer that we played ball that day, and that was how I my hair got all messed up.

I didn't want to tell her that someone had actually beaten me up, taken my things and that I would be seeing them in that person's hair the next day. And every morning was the same routine with my mother putting in more ribbons,

Finally, one day, while we shelled peas together, she began to ask me about it. I knew that I had to tell her what happened.

Afterwards I remember saying, "I *hate* her!"

"Hate?" she asked, "You're not supposed to hate anybody."

"Well," I insisted, "I hate her."

"No, no, you're not supposed to do that. I've taught you better than that.!"

Again, I said, (under my breath, because I couldn't talk back), "Well I hate *her*."

But she always knew what I was saying. This particular time, while I was holding a handful of peas, she said, "Come go with me." She told me to bring the bucket of water which we were using to rinse them.

I followed her out to a clay dirt hill where it was customary for community members to gather, eat the dirt and share bits of juicy gossip. Mom prepared to demonstrate how to plant a seed.

Clay dirt was very hard and I wondered how we were going to break it. She hit the ground with a garden hoe. It was so hard it could not be broken. Then she touched me on my chest and said, "That is how your heart is. When you hate your heart is like this hard ground."

"Now look at this water as God, and as I dig with this hoe while pouring water on it, it's like praying for those who hurt you or who trespassed against you. When you are praying that God will help the people who hurt you, you will see how He will show up for *you*."

I replied that I didn't want to do that, that I just wanted to hate her. She taught me that no matter what someone has done to you, no matter how they hurt you, it is important for you to forgive, not necessarily for them but for yourself.

I learned to sow a seed of forgiveness. I learned even in the middle of crisis and hardship, even when being bullied by forces that were stronger than me, that I could sow a prayer for them. And when I did, I would be *planting seeds today for a better tomorrow.*

This became my guiding principle throughout my life, in business, with family, in relationships, and with all that I do in life. When others have hurt me, I found the best thing to do is to pray for them. Do I always want to? Of course not; I am only human. But in my obedience, I learned to do this on a daily basis.

When life and people become overwhelming, if you pray for them, you too will be able to watch how God will show up mightily for you.

2

"IF THERE ARE TEN WOMEN IN THE ROOM,
ALWAYS BE THE LADY."

WHO CAN FIND A VIRTUOUS WOMAN? FOR HER PRICE IS FAR ABOVE RUBIES.

PROVERBS 31:10

"Thank God it's Friday!" (TGIF) was the mantra and the philosophy of a lot of the people in Caseyville, MS.

A few miles away from my childhood home, on Highway 550, there was a tavern. I think most of us refer to them as "juke joints." It was the weekend hangout in our small rural community.

It was convenient to the neighborhood because it was closer to where everyone lived than the larger variety of night spots available in Brookhaven or Natchez. Most could get there in a matter of minutes.

One reason it was so well used is that everyone there knew most everyone who went there. All were neighbors and most were family. If a person got too tipsy, it would be friend, perhaps even a relative who made sure you arrived to your safe place.

Although my mother was never an attendee of juke joints, we had family members who were. I remember watching her as she attended to one of my grandmothers who, having exhausted herself on the dance floor, and who had more than her share of alcohol, had to be cleaned up and cared for. It was not a good sight.

During one of these times, she told me to always carry myself gracefully. She'd say, "If there were ten women in the room, no matter what they were doing, when you walk in, you be the lady."

She emphasized that I should set myself apart from those activities, telling me, "Men-folk will go through many of them before getting to you. And when they do come to you, they will respect you."

Mom never wavered on displaying herself as a lady, and she led this principle by example.

3

"ALWAYS BE YOUR VERY BEST. THAT WILL BE GOOD ENOUGH."

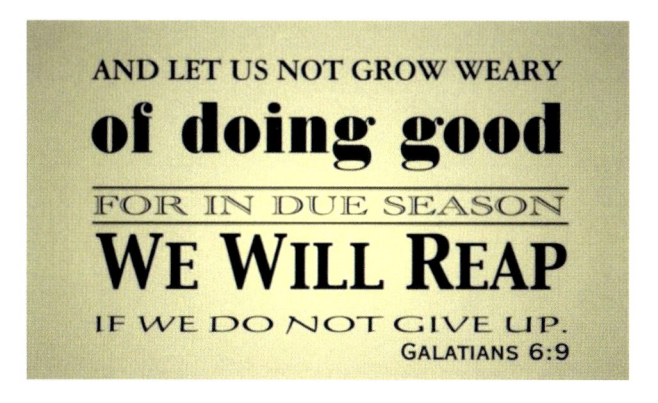

AND LET US NOT GROW WEARY **of doing good** FOR IN DUE SEASON **WE WILL REAP** IF WE DO NOT GIVE UP.
GALATIANS 6:9

As a protégé of my mother, I was always with her doing the chores. Since I was the oldest girl, and it was customary for girls to learn to cook, wash, iron, do the dishes, etc., I was always the one being called on for household, domestic duties.

It seemed that the boys always had more fun! Most of their work was outside. Plus, the games they played and the activities they participated in were not allowed for me as a daughter of Mrs. Geneva Williams.

There were times I tried to take short cuts in the work she told me to do, wanting to finish quickly. I had hopes of getting to play with my brothers outside. I did not feel like cooking in the kitchen; I wanted to make mud cakes outside. I did not want to wash clothes with a washboard in a number three galvanized tub, and then have to wring them out by hand. I wanted to swing from the ropes installed in the trees by my brothers and their friends. I would rather roll tires down the road, than to hang clothes on the line. I could hardly wait to get through working so I could go outside and get dirty.

In my haste, things just got thrown together, like the cornbread, for instance. There were times that I tried to get away with using half the ingredients, expecting the desired result. I suppose I thought it would be okay if I cut a few corners.

Those who can quickly mix up a batch of cornbread know to omit the key components is a recipe for disaster. After creating a quick mixture, putting it on the table and trying to leave, Mom would look at it, call me back, and make me do it all over again. My mom had zero tolerance for anything less than my best. She said, "Always do your very best, your very best will be good enough; and we know this is not your very best."

Once while washing clothes, she called back after I took a short cut, leaving white articles somewhat dingy. She politely asked me, "is that your very best?" She looked intently at me as though reading my heart. I couldn't lie; I knew it was not my very best. After redoing the work, she asked me again, "Is that your very best?"

I answered, "Yes ma'am."

Although my second attempt was still not quite as good as hers would have been, it was at that time my very best. When I answered that it was, she released me to play, proving to me that my very best would indeed be good enough.

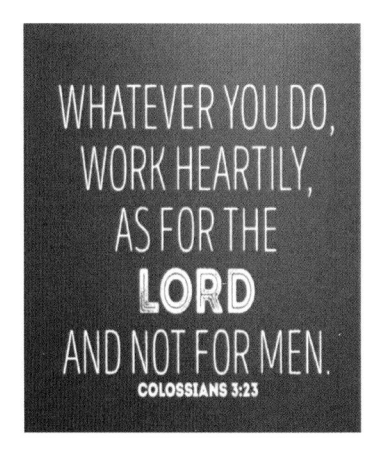

> WHATEVER YOU DO, WORK HEARTILY, AS FOR THE **LORD** AND NOT FOR MEN.
> COLOSSIANS 3:23

Even today, as I mill about working, with ministry, business, and yes, even as I yet cook and wash clothes, I still hear her voice chiding me to do and to be my very best. She taught me to put my heart into what I am doing, especially for others.

4

"STAY ON THE ROAD LESS TRAVELED BY; NOT MANY PEOPLE ARE ON THAT ROAD."

Enter through the narrow gate; for the gate is wide and the way is broad that leads to destruction, and there are many who enter through it. For the gate is small and the way is narrow that leads to life, and there are few who find it.
Matthew 7:13-14

Not everyone had transportation in our little town of Caseyville, MS. When going from one place to another, it was not uncommon to see others along the way, walking. They would walk to the store. They would walk to various creeks and springs to get water. They would walk when going to church, to visit relatives, to go to the club. People were always walking everywhere they needed to go.

As a very young girl, and countless times after, I would hear my mother say, "Take the road less traveled by" or

"Stay on the road less traveled by." She would add how not many people were on that road.

Being so young, eight or nine years of age, she was often too deep for me, and I sometimes took her advice in the literal sense. Although this bit of instruction became more clear later, at a young age, I found myself crossing over to the other side of the road when I was about to encounter other foot-traffic, like cousins, neighbors, friends and other familiar faces. So, I was obedient to be on the less-traveled side of the road.

As I grew older, however, I realized the "road" she wanted me to choose to stay on was that of always doing the right things, and for the right reasons. I was being taught to stay on the path of righteousness. This included avoiding the practice of lying, stealing and all the things that would put me on a bad path.

Over the weekends, we would see a lot of people

heading to the clubs, women in their short skirts, and the men-folk who were in hot pursuit of them. Sadly, you would see these same people later barely able to stand, much less walk.

Even my 90-pound grandmother, was barely manageable in her drunken stupor. She felt like she weighed 200 pounds as we carried the deadweight of her intoxication.

I would hear my mom say, "You don't have to do this or be this way. This is not the path that you should be on; but rather the road of love, of kindness and self-respect." She said, "You must respect yourself… if you don't, you will be just like this. So stay on the road less traveled by."

5

"ALL LADIES (THAT HAVE A HUSBAND) ARE YOUR SISTERS AND THEY SHOULD HAVE THE SAME RESPECT."

As the weekend approaches in most homes there is a growing excitement as people look forward to off-days, to getting their paychecks and to enjoying the reward of the leisure they worked hard all week for.

Within the community there was great anticipation in the air to repeat all that was done the weekend before.

But this was a very sore spot of every week in the Williams' household. In contrast, every Thursday was a time of anxiety, depression and worry. Here's why:

My dad had a best friend with whom he would hang out

from time to time. His friend's wife was also a friend to my mother. This friend and his wife often came to our home to visit my parents.

Over time, though, my dad somehow got involved with the other woman. It had gotten to the point that my dad and his friend, would actually get into a fight over this woman.

This continued for a while. At some point, a pattern was established as my dad took advantage of more opportunities to get involved with other women. Every Friday he would disappear for two days, with his paycheck. Many times some of his acquaintances would pick him up from our house.

Other times he might not even return from going to work that morning. While he was AWOL, he would be spending the bill payments and food money in his unbridled appetite for alcohol, women, and partying.

These were very sad times for my mother. Her anxiety, which started on Thursday night, had a saddening effect on us all. Her demeanor would change, knowing there were a couple of lonely days approaching; Dad would be gone, and she would be left at home with the kids.

Once, my dad did show up during the weekend; but it was only to stop by, perhaps to pick up something. However, my brother spotted and reported that another person was in the car, hiding on the floor-board. It goes without saying that this made Mom upset and very hurt. She began to cry.

Yet, she never stopped being virtuous wife and mother. She still prepared his food. She washed, dried, ironed and folded his clothes which were soiled from his weekend. She stayed faithful throughout her life, doing all that she had signed up for in their marriage. I was naive at first, not understanding the grief I saw in my mother. It became clear over time.

One day, while feeding the chickens, my mother told me, "When you get older, you're going to have men-folk in your face, because you're so pretty. They'll be trying to take you out and do certain things." She continued, "If your heart don't feel it, don't do it. Make sure that anyone coming after you is not married, because a lot of times they don't wear their rings."

"And if that man should be married or attached, you do not want to get involved with him." My mother concluded, "Whether you know the woman or not, she is still your sister. You would never do anything disrespectful to your *biological* sister; and you never do anything with any with the man of another woman because she *is* your sister."

There were many such conversations from week to week as Mom and I would be working over the weekend together. Sometimes, at dusk-dark while sitting out on the porch listening to the crickets, I would hear the chidings and wit of this virtuous, but very lonely woman.

Every time I have been approached with an offer by an attached man saying, "Baby…", it has irritated me because to this day, decades later, I can see the pain on my mother's face after many painful years of being neglected and being taken for granted.

I still hear her encouraging me, not only to avoid being the victim; but, worse, to not be a violator of this golden rule. That is, just as I would not be disrespectful to my own biological sister, I should never violate the relationship of any female. For, they too are my sisters.

6

"ALWAYS KNOW THAT WHERE THERE IS DARKNESS, I WILL MAKE SURE YOU HAVE LIGHT."

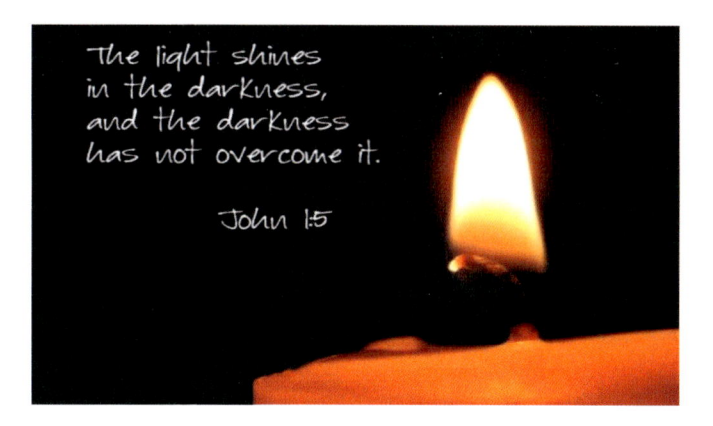

> The light shines in the darkness, and the darkness has not overcome it.
>
> John 1:5

As I think back, it seems like most of the wisdom I gained from my mother was surrounded around feeding chickens, or with her sitting on the front porch just rocking in her chair, and often, while she was combing my hair.

And I can remember long evenings when it looked like the sun would never go down. It seemed that there was sadness about something every day; especially when my mom was starting to become ill. These were times when I had to do everything!

I remember her having a conversation with me on one long night; it was so dark that I couldn't see my hand in front of my face as I was sitting there talking about it with my mom.

She said, "Yeah everything seems to be a little dark out here so we need to get up and go inside." I replied as I was getting up to go inside I remember stating again how it was, "So dark out here." She answered, "Where there is darkness, I will make sure that you have light."

I remember how that felt in my heart. Although I didn't understand it, I felt such peace as I heard those words. I wondered how, when it was so dark outside, she could make sure I have light. But as I grew older, I could remember how that happened so many times. My mom would say, "Don't be afraid; where there is darkness, I will make sure you have light."

Throughout my teen years and into my adulthood, especially when I've gone through changes, unsure of which way to go, I would remember her words. Always in some way, somehow, I would always sense her presence.

I could smell her cologne. Or while lying on the bed, it would feel like somebody sat on the side of the bed. When I looked there would be no one there. I have felt my hair move or even my face being touched. These all became assurances for me that my mother was showing me light and that it was going to be okay.

Dad's Last Birthday

One of those times occurred on my father's last birthday. A few months prior to that, we lost my uncle, Murphy, whom we called "Uncle Moon."

Uncle Moon was my dad's only sibling, and they were also best friends. They were like Mutt and Jeff, so close that if one of them was seen, the other was going to be close-by. Throughout their lives, they were always there for one another no matter what happened, even when they got angry with each other.

Uncle Moon started to get deathly ill which made my dad very sad. Dad became protective of him as he took care of him until he passed, causing my father to become depressed. I remember him being so hurt that, after my uncle passed, he moved into my uncle's bedroom just to be close to him. This continued for about two or three months, until my dad even lost the will to live his own life.

During that Christmas time, I picked him up and brought him to my house. By this time, downhearted, he too had become ill. As we neared my father's birthday, December 27th, I invited all the family, my brothers and sisters and the grands, over to my house for his birthday party. I knew my dad was growing weaker and that it was only a matter of time before we would also be losing him. He and I were excited about his birthday party.

But, this turned out to be a time of great disappointment. As Dad was experiencing one of the most grievous times in his life, none of my family came on his birthday. It wasn't that they didn't want to celebrate his birthday. But the reason given was that they didn't want to drive for an hour to visit.

One person discouraged all the others from coming, citing his anger at my bringing Dad to my house. I kept calling to see if they were coming. My questions were answered with, "It's too far for us to drive," or "I don't have the gas," or "Let's do it at a more convenient time." Two of my sisters who lived in the Jackson area, and few friends and colleagues did come. But all my dad's other children did not.

I was devastated. I remember thinking to myself, "When you are asking for money, this same one-hour distance is not an obstacle at all!" How could anyone be so selfish, knowing this would indeed be the last

Christmas and birthday this man would get to see? Is this last request, to see the whole family together, too much to ask?"

How can one person provide for ten kids all his life and not even half of them come to celebrate him this one day?

My dad's high anticipation was noticeable as his eyebrows raised every time there was a knock on my front door. And every time, I watched them fall in disappointment. He was barely able to speak at that time due to illness. So it was a struggle for him to keep asking me where everybody else was.

His questions began to stress me out because I didn't have an answer to give him that he would understand; only that they couldn't come because of other prior obligations. But, I was distraught at the look on his face, an expression of sadness that his own children didn't come.

That night I felt so bad, so depressed that I couldn't sleep. Every time I opened my eyes it felt like everything was hurting, a feeling like I've never had before! My chest ached, and my stomach was so upset that it churned.

As I went to the refrigerator to get water, the stress felt so overwhelming. I knew if I yielded to how I felt, I was literally going to die.

My mind kept saying, "Move on, persevere!" My body

got so hot with fever that I began to stagger around in the house. I remember opening the back door, standing in the midnight air trying to cool myself off. I didn't want to awaken my dad because I didn't want him to see me in that state and start to worry. So I kept very quiet and I went out on the patio.

Gripped with fear, I staggered back inside and cut out the lights in the living room, leaving the house pitch dark. Back in my dark bedroom, I knelt down on my knees with my face pressed into the floor and started praying.

I cried out, "Lord please help me! Lord don't let me die!" I repeated, "Oh God! Lord please don't let me die, not while my father is here!" (I didn't want him to be hurt at my passing). I remember lying out on the floor, still crying out to the Lord.

While I was yet going through this, in a room pitch black with darkness, a shiny glow under my bed caught my attention. I looked in the direction under the bed. There was an object, a small piece of something, that appeared to be lit. The more I looked at it, the more it radiated. When I moved my head back and forth, the more the small glow stared

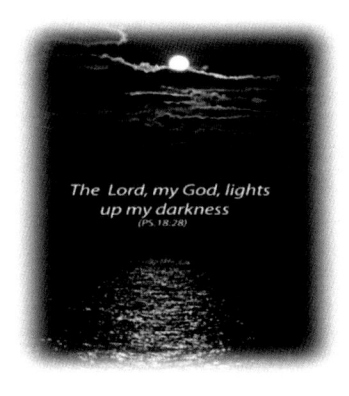

The Lord, my God, lights up my darkness
(PS. 18:28)

and shined right back at me.

Something about the light began to bring relief. My head began to feel a little better. Immediately, I remembered the words of my mother: "There will be darkness, but I will make sure that you have light." I remember saying, "Mom, you haven't left me!" I said, "Lord, thank you! Thank you Jesus! Thank you!"

I looked again at this little light under the bed, shining on me, wondering what it actually was. I managed to get up and turn on the light. I remember using a broom to sweep the light from under the bed.

And there it was; a battery which had come out from the back of one of my watches. I don't know how it found its way underneath the bed. But it appeared to be propped up on something. I could see the light, just a little light, shining on me. That small glow, so tiny, so shiny, gave me hope!

To this day I know that my mother watches over me and I know that she watches and takes care of me. Every time I have had darkness, light has always come to shine on me.

Another "Geneva"

Once, I was having a very rough day, feeling hurt and disappointed. My spirit was compelling me to go into Burlington's. I did not want nor did it need to shop for anything. Sometimes, I can be hard headed. But this time my spirit kept prompting me to go. And so I went.

There, I met a nice, very friendly lady. And we just started talking. It was interesting, because she said that she didn't know why she came into the store either. But, like me, her mind kept telling her to come inside of Burlington's.

During our lengthy conversation about clothes, children, and products in the store, I found out she was from out of town. She was ahead of me as we each checked out and prepared to leave.

Personally, I was still having a rough day. But, as we walked out, this lady said, "I have talked to you for almost 30 minutes and I don't even know your name."

I answered, "My name is Kolean Sanders."

Then she said, "My name is Geneva Washington."

Of course, this brought tears to my eyes. When she asked me the reason for my tears, I told her, "Because my mother's name is Geneva, and she has passed." We hugged and held onto each other as a peace came over me.

Geneva Washington has become a dear friend and over the years as we have had frequent talks. From the brief, chance encounter, on a very bad day, I listened and obeyed my spirit. In doing so, I have forged a life-long friendship with another Geneva, who like my own mother, followed God's leading to be a blessing for a total stranger. I am ever so grateful.

There have been so many things my mother told me that have been confirmed and have come true. I am ever most thankful to God for my mother, Mrs. Geneva Williams.

7

"YOU WILL GIVE AWAY MONEY, HOUSES, CARS, JEWELRY, AND CLOTHES; YOUR CUP WILL RUN OVER."

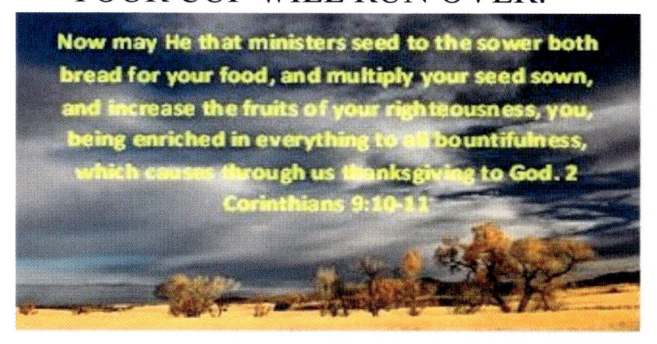

> Now may He that ministers seed to the sower both bread for your food, and multiply your seed sown, and increase the fruits of your righteousness, you, being enriched in everything to all bountifulness, which causes through us thanksgiving to God. 2 Corinthians 9:10-11

There were many times when my mother and I hung clothes on the line together. Sometimes she pulled me aside and sat me down for a bit of prophetic encouragement. I often found myself listening to her foretell of the many situations which I would experience later on in my life.

These weighty discussions were often centered around

chickens. That's right; chickens. She was always able to somehow relate my life to these creatures which often found themselves on the dinner plates of the Williams' household. I remember thinking, "I don't want to be like nor live the life of these seemingly mindless barnyard birds."

She would point out, however, how some of the birds were always scratching and clawing at the dirt seeking food; or pecking, raking the grass and sand, eating anything and everything that could be passed off as food.

But then, there were those chickens that were not in the rat race, so to speak. They just watched the others' feeding frenzy, competing for the same few dusty specks of cornbread crumbs, ants and even the fecal matter of their friends, and never truly having enough.

Mom said people were the same way. Some claw scratch and grind, exerting all their effort to out-eat the others, always waiting and hoping for more.

There was always a group of chickens who appeared to oversee the activity of the dependent cacklers. "This group has learned to find food on their own." She said, "They were taught early how to go and get it without having to wait for it to be brought to them."

She would go on to make statements about my destiny.

The trouble I had with this activity is that, for a person who had grown up in very rustic surroundings, and having not seen much else but that type of existence, some of what she shared with me was foreign. Some things simply could not be understood from the standpoint of young a girl living out in the rural parts of Lincoln County, Mississippi.

So, when she told me I would give away money, it didn't make a lot of sense. We barely had enough for ourselves; certainly not enough to give any away.

When my mom said I would give away houses, I could not very easily get my mind around this whole notion of providing housing for someone else, especially when we didn't have a nice house of our own.

For someone who barely had reliable transportation for a household of twelve, it sounded like a dream to hear that I would be giving away cars. I could more easily see being in a position to perhaps give someone a ride to their destination.

Even the jewelry and clothes items that she claimed I would give seemed a little off-kilter of the realities that I knew.

It wasn't that I had a hard time believing I would have a charitable heart; because Mom always set a strong example of this. She often prepared food for total strangers passing along the way. She was always sowing into the lives of others with her meager resources. It was simply the magnitude of giving that she prophesied over me that I was having the hardest time seeing.

But as time would tell, and as fate would have it, I have been positioned to do all of what she declared and much more. I have been blessed to buy and give away many cars and several houses, many expensive outfits and lots of fine jewelry.

The legacy she imparted to me included the act of giving and sowing; but the *level* of my sowing that she decreed and declared has been proven many times over as I have been in a position to share with others as my mother predicted.

The Lord has been faithful, always providing seed to the sower.

Glory to God!

8

"WALK FOR YOUR BROTHERS AND SISTERS,
UNTIL THEY CAN WALK FOR THEMSELVES."

As my mom's health began to deteriorate, we would have a lot of heart-to-heart talks. She would insert into the conversations small, subtle clues about the possibility of not always being around for me. Although we were having these talks, I still had no idea she was purposely sharing with me to prepare me for the role I would have to assume in her absence.

I distinctly remember one night in her hospital room. She covered a lot during this particular one-to-one talk.

I pulled up a chair to her bedside and lay my head across her body, while she stroked my hair. When I looked up at her, I saw her eyes overflow with tears that streamed down her face.

Mom asked me, "Do you remember how I showed you how to cook?" When I answered yes, she said, "You are going to have to learn to do that for your brothers; they are going to need you. And life is going to be difficult for you all. "Since you are the oldest girl," she continued, "I need you to take care of them. I need you to walk for your brothers and sisters until they can walk for themselves."

In my reply to her, I said, "I don't understand what all that means, where are *you* going?"

She said, "Well, I may not always be here, and I need you to promise me that you will watch out for your brothers and sisters."

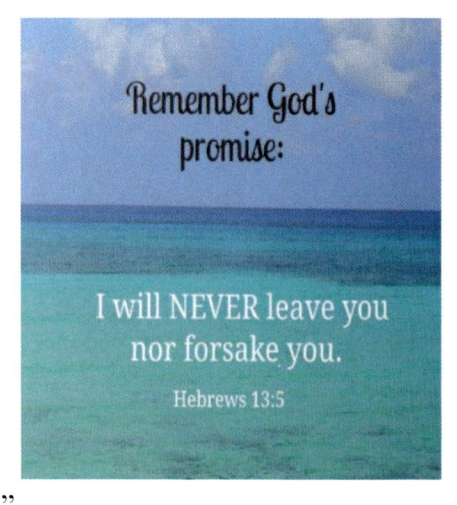

Of course, I said, "Yes ma'am, I'll watch out for them."

She could clearly see my fear. She said, "Always know

even if I'm not here in the flesh, I am here in spirit.

My mother was not your typical super saint who attended church three of four times a week. She passed onto me her best knowledge about God, which she had inherited from my grandmother. Yet, one of the very last things she said to me was this:

"I regret that I didn't teach you more about God, and that I didn't take you to church more often." She said, "I wish I had spent more time teaching from the bible."

I could see her anguish at this fact. It was the final chat that we would have; because she would pass away that night.

As a young girl, it became clear almost immediately what she was trying to tell me all those times in private conversation, those times when I felt she was being hard on me. She was actually preparing me to walk in her shoes, to take care of the household, to do all that she had done for her family, to fulfill her calling as a parent, often without any appreciation or reward.

The lot fell on me to be the mother, and to experience the parental sense of responsibility for providing, protecting, cleaning, feeding, nurturing and training Mom's children.

I felt such fear, anxiety, and panic at the realization of this new burden. It was so overwhelming that I would become nauseated and would throw up. This would later include the grief my mother would have felt at the loss of three of my four deceased brothers.

I could barely sleep at night knowing that at or before the break of day, I needed to prepare breakfast and get clothes and the family ready to go to school. I would wake up running.

Even while in school, I knew at the end of the day, I would have to wash clothes, cook for the family, and get the house cleaned. All the chores that I previously felt I was being mistreated with actually became the very things for which I had been prepared. These tasks trained me to hold our family together.

Driven to fulfill my promise, I was given God's grace to endure the hard work, the many grievous challenges, and so much shame.

As a Christian, I am reminded how Jesus commissioned His disciples on what to do and what to expect upon His departure. He closed with, "Lo I am with you always even until the end of the world." He promised the grace they needed to walk it out.

My mother, Geneva Williams, shared parting words charging me to fulfill the work she started in our family within her short span of life. She closed with, "Always know that, even if I'm not here in the flesh, I am with you in spirit."

Other council and instructions which Mom gave me

during this and other conversations are covered in full account in the book *Where There is Darkness, There will be Light.*

9

"BE CAREFUL OF YOUR TONGUE. IT'S LIKE A SHARP KNIFE. ONCE YOU CUT SOMEONE, THE HEALING WILL TAKE TIME,OR, THE WOUND MAY BE TOO DEEP TO HEAL."

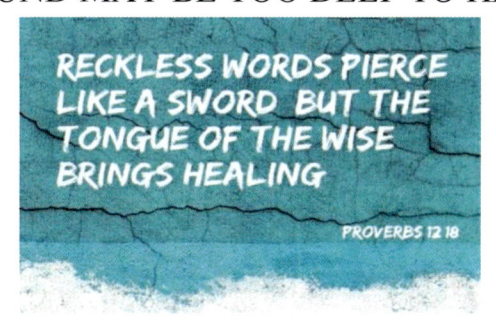

> RECKLESS WORDS PIERCE LIKE A SWORD BUT THE TONGUE OF THE WISE BRINGS HEALING
>
> PROVERBS 12 18

There was a time when I felt mistreated, even hated. It seemed like of all the hard work which needed to be done, I was the first one to be called on, if not the *only* one.

My big strong brothers would be right there when there was a call for firewood for warmth or cooking. It was necessary for it to be hauled inside, handy for the next day.

I was called to get the clothes off the line, to go and fold all the clothes, to go and bring water from the springs around the way, and to have that number three wash tube filled.

I remember a growing resentment in the fact that all the boys were usually right there. I thought to myself, "Why are you making me do all of this, and why aren't you getting them to do some of the work?"

Once, when I was walking away from my mother, I was angry and fussing to myself. It was a high crime in those days to talk back to parents, or any adult for that matter. So anything spoken disrespectfully better not be heard!

"You make me sick," I whispered under my breath.

I will never forget the look on Mom's face when I said that. Even though I said it with a barely audible mumble, she partly heard me and partially read my lips as she saw my reflection in a nearby mirror.

The expression she wore on her face was a combination of hurt, surprise, and disappointment. She looked at me and said, "One day I won't be here to make you sick."

A couple of weeks later, while she was yet pouring into me, sharing wisdom with me, and loving me, I became filled with sorrow about what I said. So, I went to her and said that my heart hurts.

She asked me why, in a very caring way. "Why does your heart hurt?"

My answer: Because you heard what I said, and I didn't mean that."

Mom said, "You should never say anything that you don't mean. You never know the hurt that you can cause." She went on, "Your tongue can be as sharp as a knife. Once you cut someone, you cause pain. Sometimes they get over it; but sometimes they never get over it. You can cut so deep with the tongue that the wound may never heal"

Then she followed with, "But I forgive you."

I replied, "Ma'am?"

She repeated that she had forgiven me. Finally she told me, "One day you will understand why I'm doing what I'm doing."

In time, I would understand that she was doing what she felt she must do in order to pass the baton of responsibility on to a very young lady. I would have to bear the sole responsibility of raising the keeping the children and managing the house she was soon to leave behind.

Mom was also right about the pain that the tongue can cause. Although I am grateful for her forgiveness, even to this day, every time I think about it, it hurts.

She talked about how the pain of a spoken word can hurt others, but I discovered it can also hurt the one who spoke it out. She said the hurt can be so deep and so permanent that is may not heal. I didn't realize that the one who could hurt the most, for the longest period, could, in fact, be the one who actually misused the tongue to cause a wound to another.

I still feel the impact of this lesson from my mother.

10

"LISTEN TO GOD WHEN HE SPEAKS TO YOU. DO WHAT GOD SAYS AND DON'T BE AFRAID."

Saturday was our day for washing clothes, hanging them on the clothesline, cooking, and washing my hair. Afterwards, I would sit on the front porch with my mother.

One time while combing my hair, she stopped abruptly, jumped up and said, "Well I got go!" She quickly ran into the kitchen and began to make peanut butter sandwiches, putting them in a bag with a jar of water.

Afterwards, she came back outside and waited. I asked her, "Why did you do that?"

She would simply smile and answer, "We have company coming."

"How do you know that?", I asked.

She replied by saying, "My spirit tells me that someone will need food and water to drink so I am obeying my spirit. It is an emotion that God puts into your body to do good."

I asked her, "What does it feel like?"

She laughed and said, "It's like being very thirsty and drinking a cold glass of water."

I asked, "Would I ever want that type of water?"

Again she laughed and said, 'You already have it!"

One day, after seeing this happen many times, and having this same conversation with her, I asked, "How can I do that?"

My mom said, "You have to listen to God when he speaks to you."

My next question was, "And how do you do that?"

She answered, "You have to say, 'What do you want me to do for someone else today? That's what you say."

I can remember many times when my mother would get up, running to meet people who showed up out of nowhere. As a little girl, I thought about how powerful that must be.

One morning, I asked God what I could do for someone else? And nothing happened. This occurred three or four different times. And each time nothing happened. This hurt my feelings. I told my mom what I did and how nothing had happened. I asked again how she did this.

Mom simply smiled and said, "You don't mean it."

I quickly said, "Yes I do!"

Mom told me to be very quiet. "Ask God for what you want. And He will give it to you because you asked for it."

So a few days later I said to God "Help me to help someone else." Then again, "Help me to help someone else! This time there was a feeling inside that was different. This went on for months, this different sort of feeling down on the inside.

Finally, one day, I had this burst of energy that wouldn't let me go. Suddenly I started to cry. So I ran to my mother and told her, "Dad is coming! Dad is coming!

She replied, "No, he won't. He won't be here until Saturday; this is Thursday!"

I said "No, he *is* coming, I hear him! He's coming. I feel it. It feels just like I'm very thirsty, and, I am wanting a cold drink of water!"

I felt it that time, and I knew that God was talking to me. After that happened several more times, I started to have the same feelings my mother was having, at the same times.

My mother was so proud she would always say, "Just wait on God. Listen! There's always a lesson when He talks to you. You will always know when things will happen before they happen. Just stay in line with God and He will speak to you."

Through the years, as I have learned to wait, listen, and obey God, I have seen Him work in some of the most amazing ways. A lot of those times He would speak to my spirit just before something would occur, sometimes very good things, sometimes very bad.

Quite a few of those times I shared with others. When the things God showed me happened, the people I told are either celebrating or grieving, depending on what the situation may have been.

I am not surprised because He will have already shown me and prepared me in the spirit.

11

"YOU WILL MEET PEOPLE MANY, MANY YEARS LATER WHO WILL REMIND YOU OF THESE CONVERSATIONS - IN WORDS, PICTURES OR A SMILE. THEY WILL LOOK IN YOUR EYES AND SAY, 'WOW!' AND YOU WILL FEEL MY PRESENCE."

My mother used to say I am always watching over you in spirit, even if I've gone away.

So many times she would tell me that if she was not here with me, someone would give me confirmation of things that we talked about many years before. In my life today, this happens over and over again.

I remember going to Dallas, Texas seeking to buy a security firm from a gentleman there. He was sick at that time and had postponed several scheduled meetings. We would call him frequently just to have conversations.

One day his wife called me saying that he was out of the hospital, and asking if we would come back to

Dallas. When we returned however, he was still very under-the-weather and did not want to talk. We did not want this to be yet another wasted trip. So, finally, I built up the nerve to call him.

He complained, "I don't have time to talk to you right now young lady. It has to be another time! Did you get the information that I sent by my wife?"

I answered, "Yes I did. But we have travelled to see you, maybe three or four times, and you always cancel the appointment. Please keep in mind that we are traveling by air fare from Jackson Mississippi, and it is getting very expensive!"

He replied, "Well maybe another time, or the next time."

I began to debate about how much it cost to come back and forth with wasted trips. I questioned if this deal was something that he wanted to do or not. "Please just say yay or nay."

He aggravated me with a response of 'Maybe.'

I got off the phone with him hoping he would call me back. I waited about 45 minutes and decided once again to call him.

Before I did, I reflected on how my mother said,

"Always be humble, always be kind, speak in a soft tone of kindness, but always be the blessing."

When I called him back, he answered the phone shouting. "What!!!"

I politely said, "Hi, I'm Kolean Sanders. I'm with SanJo Security Services. And I know that you have been under the weather. Please let me apologize for inconveniencing you by this call." I followed with, "Let me give you the reason that I'm so persistent."

"When I spoke to your wife, she was so excited for me to meet such a special husband. We talked many times about how great you are, how in your business, so many people respect you. Your wife told me that you were the first black US Marshall in the state of Texas to do so many great things, including your being first to change some of the laws, and to do so much for minorities in business."

"I was so excited to hear a woman speak so well about her husband that I just wanted to meet you, to say hello. I told your wife that I could hardly wait to meet this wonderful man!"

"Now I know that it has been a long day for you. But if you could kindly give me about 30 minutes of your time, I would appreciate it so much. It's about six hours before my flight leaves and I would really, really appreciate just being able to listen to your story."

I threw in, "I'm sure that you know as a woman-owned business, it is very difficult to even get into the arena that you are in at this time. So I would be so grateful for just 30 minutes of your time. "

He said thanks for all of the accolades, but that it would still have to be another time. We ended the call with me being humble and grateful for the conversation we just had. I remember looking at my phone counting, "1, 2, 3, 4, 5" And, shortly after getting to 5, my phone rang.

It was the Texan. "Miss Sanders?", he said in a low voice, "Can you be here at 6 o'clock? I will give you 30 minutes and 30 minutes only."

When I arrived, I stepped on the front step. Immediately, I started to cry. I could feel something extremely powerful on the other side of the door, so much so, that when I got to it, I wasn't sure I wanted to go through the door.

His wife answered the doorbell and told us to come in. My business partner and I introduced ourselves to them as they offered us chairs.

He had been bed-ridden in the hospital, and had a bag of what seemed like 50 bottles of medication. Yet, in spite of his illness, this man was so full of life! He had a wife that loved him so much. It was just unbelievable, how much she respected him. I could hardly wait to hear what he had to say.

He had made a list of things to talk about; all of the positive things that he had done with his company. He shared about the how his company was growing, the many contracts he had, and the great number of people who saw him as the only one they trusted. I sat there on the edge of my seat feeling so excited for him and his accomplishments.

Then he shifted the conversation. "Enough about me," he said, "Let's talk about you some."

I start talking to him about our company. My business partner expressed to him how he heard the man was retiring, that he wanted to sell his company, and how we desired to purchase it. We expressed our love for his company's history, and that we definitely wanted to be a part of that history.

So the meeting that started out for scheduled for only 30 minutes turned into over three hours of intriguing conversation.

Suddenly he stopped talking and began to just stare at me. He then told me that I was the person who had been in his dreams. He said, "I have been dreaming about this lady, and I don't understand why. I would dream and I would give my daughter parts of the story. She's an artist, and she would start to draw."

He said that on many occasions he had dreamt about that very moment. He did not know who the lady was in his dreams, but that she just kept 'bothering' him in his dreams. Then he noted how I had been so persistent to see him.

He looked at me and he said, "I know why I was dreaming. I have to give you something." He shared with me two pictures, the artwork his daughter had done in her illustration of the dreams as he had conveyed them to her.

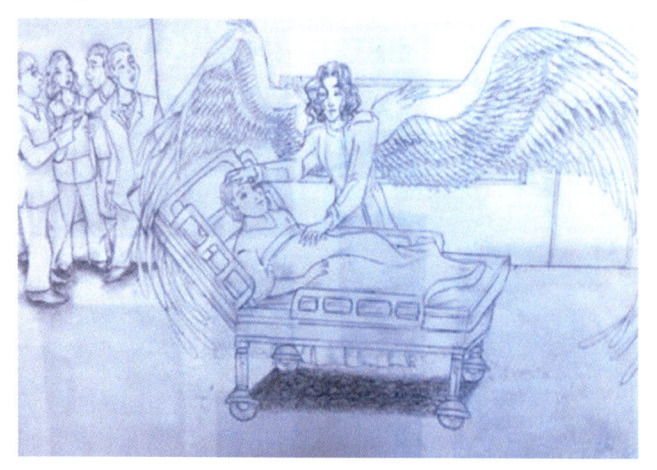

One of the pictures was of me, when I was a little girl, when my mom was dying. I was standing by her bed. I remember finally kneeling by her bed and I putting my face on her leg while her doctors were standing at the door. She told me angels were coming, and they were going to take care of me.

In this picture, everything was just like I remember, it when my mother and I had our last conversation. It was at the time when I finally realized my mother was going to die and that I would probably never see her again.

The other picture was of a big board room. Seated at the huge board table were men and women. A very large angel with a huge wingspan hovered the room in a protective posture, caring for the people at the board table.

This picture confirms and reminds me of what my mother said when she told me, "You will have many companies. You will be sitting with kings, and you will go places that you never thought you would go."

Again my mother was right. I have sat at the table with kings, ambassadors, and vice presidents of other countries.

Today, those pictures are on the walls in all of my

offices. Each one of them has a special meaning and occupies a space in my heart. Because of these gifts, this gentleman will likewise always be a special part of my life experience.

When visiting hours were over that day in Dallas, it was so difficult to leave and to go home.

Two weeks after the visit in Dallas, his wife called to tell us that he was back in hospital. I returned to Texas to visit him while he was there. Shortly thereafter he passed.

As I look at those pictures now, I often think of how over 40 plus years later, my mother is still keeping her promises. People still confirm and validate many of her words and predictions, in conversations, pictures, and people.

People sometimes say, "There is something very special about you." (I hear that a lot). I simply smile and say to myself, "My mother said you would say that."

And then I say, "Thanks Mom, for planting so many seeds, so much wisdom, for so many days, for my better tomorrow."

12

CONCLUSION

Many times in life, it is important to have a mentor, someone who has, as the old folks say, been where we are trying to go. We find these people in church or school, sometimes even on television screens. I was fortunate to find a true mentor in my mother.

Every one of us has or had a mother. We glean from them what we need to survive and to thrive. Mother wit and intuition, indeed has saved a lot of lives.

I would like to take a moment to encourage you to reflect on your memories, good and bad. Ponder even the miracle that resulted in your being here.

No matter your opinion of the household in which you were raised, nor your ideology on parenting, you are in control of the honor you can give to the parent (s) who raised you, whether or not they remain with you.

Embrace the wisdom of your predecessors. Cherish the experiences that give you the opportunity to apply their principles. In doing this you make your parents, your mentors and guardians immortal. Let it, then, become part of the legacy you either start or continue as you plant seeds today for your better tomorrow.

ABOUT THE AUTHOR

The late Mrs. Geneva Williams predicted many hardships that her daughter, "young Kolean," would face after her departure, when Kolean was only 16 years old. She also made a dying request of Kolean that she would "walk" for her remaining brothers and sisters until they could walk for themselves."

In an effort to equip her daughter-protégé, Mrs. Williams also shared vital gems of wisdom and sundry maxims. These concepts would later become the fuel for Kolean's very survival.

As a youngster, traumatic events occurred over several years, transforming Kolean Sanders' childhood into one of shame, bitterness and pain. She carried within the wounds of these devastating changes throughout her life.

At one point, as a teenager, filled with anguish, she decided to end her life. Obviously, however, God had another plan and did not allow her suicide attempt to be successful.

Instead, she became a fighter and began to focus on her commitment to fulfill her final mother's final request. Geneva's legacy empowered Kolean to survive and emerge as a towering overcomer today. She attributes her survival and success to God's grace and the nurture of her dear mother, Mrs. Geneva Williams. Kolean is also the author of her autobiography *Where there is Darkness, there will be Light*, currently being published. This book includes more details on the life and the legacy of her mother. She also shares openly about her life, the struggles she faced, and her journey from victim to victor.

Kolean currently resides in Jackson, MS and she is the founder of the Geneva Foundation, Inc. a nonprofit organization which empowers and meets the broad spectrum of recovery needs for those who have suffered abuse.

She is a dynamic speaker that moves all audiences to tears as well as inspires thousands to choose life after abuse.

Geneva's House

Headquarters of

The Geneva Foundation

A Nonprofit Organization

Founded in honor of Mrs. Geneva Williams

Support the cause of recovery after abuse with the Geneva Foundation, Inc.
Contact
601-501-1587
Or go to
www.genevafoundationinc.org

A registered 501©(3)

All proceeds from the sale of this booklet as well as donation are tax deductible and are used to support the mission of
The Geneva Foundation.

Kolean W Sanders,

Business owner, Author, Speaker, Trainer, Facilitator, Founder of the Geneva Foundation

For speaking engagements

Call 601-738-6339

Made in the USA
Columbia, SC
27 June 2019